21ST CENTURY SLAVE

Road to financial freedom

ARITZ GÓMEZ LARROSA

Copyright © 2019 Aritz Gómez Larrosa

All rights reserved.

DEDICATION

I dedicate this book to my daughter and my son; they have been the inspiration that has motivated me to write and to be able to shape in some way the desire of wanting to help others.

To my parents and my sister, thank you. Thank you for giving me the necessary tools that have made me the man I am today.

And especially thank you to my wife, who has always been by my side supporting me unconditionally, has trusted in me and in everything I have set out to achieve.

DEDICATION iii

BOOK i

1 PROLOGUE: 1

2 INTRODUCTION: 3

3 FINANCIAL EDUCATION 8

4 MY APPALLING ECONOMIC MANAGEMENT .. 12

5 HOW I ACQUIRED BAD DEBTS AND FORGOT THE GOOD 14

6 EMOTIONS AND MONEY 19

7 HOW TO MANAGE YOUR INCOME BETTER 22

How to eliminate debt: 23

Savings Methods: 27

Investment: 32

8 TOWARDS FINANCIAL FREEDOM 39

9 SUMMARY OF CONCEPTS: 42

10 RECOMMENDATIONS: 46

ABOUT THE AUTHOR 48

BOOK

This book is also in digital format, if you are a reader on ebook devices or other electronic media on the AMAZON WEBSITE, you will be able to purchase it.

You will also find it both on paper and in digital format on the different amazon websites in multiple countries where this company is established.

This book was published and printed both digitally and on paper in 2019.

1 PROLOGUE:

A few years ago, after 6 hours of sleep, like any other day, I woke up early to go to work. I took a shower, had breakfast, got dressed and rushed out to get the car. There was almost always traffic on the way to work. I had a steady job, and as the months and years went by, I was getting more and more annoyed to get stuck in traffic.

It was then, with the daily endless congestion, that an idea that came to mind changed my life forever. Suddenly, while a commercial song was playing on the radio, that I wasn't even listening to, a light bulb went on in my head. What I wondered at that moment was, for how long did I wanted to continue that lifestyle. Don't get me wrong, I had a very decent life, a beautiful family, good friends, a well-paid job (not a big salary but above average), I had always felt very loved and fortunately I did not lack anything basic to live, I even had "extras things", things that when I was little I dreamed of having. Maybe too many...and to be completely honest, more than I could actually afford to own. So I decided that I had to make a change in my life, I had thousands of thoughts and emotions running through my head, I was fed up and angry, and I realized that I had been deceived, that I had been taught from a young age to reach a lifestyle that implies to be "tied up" everywhere. Anchored to a job, working for others, depending on a salary, which even not being bad, could vanish overnight. What made me most angry was believing that this lifestyle was a wonderful thing, that working so hard for a long time would dignify me. And probably for many it is, it's very respectable and I don't criticize it at all, but for me, on the contrary it was nothing wonderful. I was trapped in a system that I didn't know how to escape.

2 INTRODUCTION:

The purpose of this book is to optimize our private economy and improve our economic health by using personal finance techniques. It is designed for anyone who wants to take the path to financial freedom. It explains the beginnings clearly and easily and how to start and achieve that goal. It is a basic and very practical guide where I explain in three steps how to get to achieve it. I will briefly summarize it to give you an idea. First, all kinds of debts must be eliminated. Second, specific savings plans must be implemented. And third, how to invest part or all of those savings so they will pay off.

Before I go into matters, I would like to clarify two things; What is the meaning of financial freedom in a large scale and the sense of slavery I refer in my book. There are many definitions and meanings about financial freedom, but from my point of view, the one who defines and explains it with very good judgment is **Esmeralda Gómez López,** an intelligent and brilliant woman in every way whom I deeply admire and I am extremely grateful for all she has provided me. When we talk about financial freedom, we can define it as our economic situation in which it would not be necessary to work to receive an income. An optimal state financially speaking at a particular level, in which you can live without worrying at any time about money. That means that each person's financial freedom may be different from one another (it will always depend on each person's needs). To sum up, you can say that you are financially free when you can stop working because it's no longer necessary, as your sources of income are enough to cover everything you need.

On the other hand, when looking for the meaning of the word slave, we will basically find three definitions.

- The first; A person who lacks freedom and self-rights because they are subject to the will and dominance of another person who is their owner and who can buy or sell them as if it were a commodity. But it's not this definition I refer to in my story.
- The second definition is that person who is dominated by a passion or a vice that is needed to live or feel good. But this definition isn't the one I'm talking about either.
- The third meaning and this is the reason for the title of the book, is that

person who, of its own will or necessity, is constantly responsible for a duty or obligation, such as work.

This is where I want to emphasize, we are slaves to our jobs, we have been taught and programmed for it, they have instilled in us that we have to work a lot and hard to get to have more, but nothing further from reality. The majority of the population is subject to this system, and I include myself. We are tied to low-paid work, sacrificing countless hours and forcing us to set aside our family reconciliations, our leisure time and ultimately our true freedom.

With this I do not want you to understand that we do not have to work to achieve our goals, we must do so and with great care and dedication. This will honor us as a person, bring us satisfaction, and we will be proud of the outcome of our efforts. But that doesn't mean we have to work for others at any price. If you decide to do so, well, I respect it and even more because I, at the time, also decided to do it. But it was enough, I started working for myself, in addition to keeping my job, and that's how I started my path to financial freedom.

My wish is to be able to help others who have somehow been involved in the same situation as me, wanting to change toxic habits in their lives on a financial level that can influence the rest of their lives. Or much better, not to get to where I fell and avoid to get to this point. This would be ideal.

I want to tell you that you are not alone and there is a good chance of getting a solution in case you find yourself in a situation that you want to change. There are many techniques with which to reduce your debts, save, and generate income. If you want to improve your life, start by improving your financial health and you will realize how all the rest improves progressively, believe me, I have been able to check it out for myself. I'm an ordinary man in the society I live in, standard model if you want to call it that way. I have a wife and children. I have a mortgage, car, loans, common expenses and so on... But what I will explain is applicable to anyone, in any situation, regardless of their family, economic or social situation.

I will teach you how I have come to change my financial situation and how this has completely changed my life for the better, in every way. If you find yourself in a precarious work situation, you don't like what you do and you're in debt, here you'll find a guide on how to change that, how to get out of that loop if you really want to. Or at least, solve some of the issues. It's working for me. I'm a simple person who comes from a humble family, so if I've been able to do it, you can get it too. I'm totally convinced that you can because I've done it, and I'm no better or smarter than you. So now convince yourself and do it. Over time you will see that it will have been one of the best decisions you will have made in your life.

3 FINANCIAL EDUCATION

I cannot speak of financial education without naming Robert Kiyosaki, who with his work "Rich dad, Poor dad" clearly explains what it is and the importance of it. One of the definitions, among others, of financial education is the following: it is the ability to understand how money works in the world, how a person gets it (makes money), administers it, invests it, and donates it to help others. More specifically, financial education refers to the set of skills and knowledge that allow an individual to make informed decisions of all their financial resources.

Obviously each and every one of us has been influenced by our education, the schools where we have studied, activities that we have carried out, the kind of culture to which we belong, possibly a religious background, the family environment and friendships, in short, we have a greater or lesser socialization and in a unique and different environment for each one. However, generally speaking and in most developed countries, the educational structure is usually similar, we go to school from a young age, followed by a higher education until we get to university, choosing a type of training depending on the career path we want to achieve in the future. It is also true that this path is not always followed by all, sometimes for different reasons, many do not finish high school and never mind higher education. Which I consider a mistake, not because of following these trends, but because training is essential in order to think and act for yourself. Whatever that training is, it doesn't necessarily have to be a traditional academic education. Training yourself and learning is extremely essential, whether it is in what we like and we are passionate about or in what we believe will lead us to achieve our best goals. Unfortunately, the vast majority have not been trained in financial education, vital to living a healthy life on an economic level.

Many might tell me that it is very easy to blame the system, society in general, the family, etc... And they would be quite right, because the easy thing is not to admit our own mistakes. The easy thing is to blame others, randomly or by chance, and that's why we live the life we live. But let me tell you one thing, in fact the sole owners of our decisions, our choices, our successes and our mistakes, we are ourselves, just us and no one but us.

I have to confess that until I realized this and accepted it, I didn't start moving forward. So, decide for yourself, make your own choices and be consistent with them. It doesn't matter if you hit or fail, what matters is that you, just you, decide to really have complete control over your life in a real way. It's the only way to move forward, thrive and reach your own goal. In my case, that goal is to achieve financial freedom in its fullness. Let me tell you now that it has been one of the best decisions I've ever made, that's with determination and absolute commitment. I could lie to you and tell you it's easy, but it's not, it takes effort and dedication on a daily basis, but it is really worth it, more than you can imagine.

As for me, I'm not a money guru, I'm not an expert broker, and I'm not a millionaire. I haven't written famous books about how to get rich, like Napoleon Hill, Robert Kiyosaki or other great ones. I am only a humble worker, for the time being employed by others, who wishes to achieve financial freedom. I'm on my way and I'm going to get it, so if you want you can also do it. You have to consider that, think, and do it.

I invite you to implement my formula, the one that has really worked for me. I have called it formula R. L. T. A. (Read, Learn, Think and Act). Learn, train yourself, and invest in financial education, that's all. You'll be investing in yourself, to improve your life and improve as a person. In addition to investing in yourself, you'll be doing it for your family and environment. Nobody is going to do it in your behalf, only you can decide. But I can assure you that if you do, you will never regret it and will feel fulfilled and satisfied by your efforts and your accomplishments. I want you to achieve your economic goals, to learn more about the importance of a good financial education. I want you to grow as a person in the finance field, which will therefore give you experience and not only you will have more money, but you will have matured and evolved in all aspects. Money matters, yes. It is true that it does not bring happiness, but it helps to achieve it. I had been taught, maybe like you, that money is not important, but it is. Not to become obsessed about it or a tight-fisted person because that's not happiness, nor is it profitable if you don't move and invest your money. What is clear is that whatever situation comes our way, it is not the same to face it with money than without it. So, get training and invest in financial education, I can't tell you any clearer.

4 MY APPALLING ECONOMIC MANAGEMENT

I want to explain to you my experience, my bad experience, to warn you of what can happen if you manage your economy badly. In case you're at a similar point, you'll have to start from scratch like I had to do. In my defense, it is that I did poor economic management because I had not been financially educated. It's just one part of the blame, the other part was my thoughts and my bad economic habits. I hope you're on time, and if you're reading this book it's already a big step, it means you've already started to educate yourself financially. Congratulations!

Regarding my income, I earned it exclusively through my work. Paid employment, which means, working for someone else. I have to say that I had a decent salary and the schedule was not at all outrageous, so I could not complain much. I considered myself lucky taking into account the difficult times. Even so, my only source of income was badly managed. As a start, I had almost no savings and this was a very serious mistake. In addition, having a permanent contract, I had no major obstacles as a borrower and the banks provided and granted me loans. With this I began to do what I thought was logical, borrowing money to pay for things, such as a mortgage for the house, a car loan, furniture loans, financing electronic products, etc... I didn't lose my mind though, I looked at interest rates and if I had the chance to get a zero-interest rate, I took advantage of it. But over time, what seemed to me to be a fabulous idea, ended up not being that great. On the other hand, I had no choice as I believed that otherwise I could not afford having nice things. The fact is, after accumulating multiple loans and credits, which were being granted to me without problem, it turned out that my only source of income, my payroll, was almost inexistent after paying for all my loans and fees. And I had little left for the rest of the stuff. I had the essential to cover basic needs but it was increasingly difficult to cover them. Extremely terrible management I have to admit, and it was getting bigger and bigger, almost without realizing it. It was a gradual situation and I didn't realize the problem I was generating. When I became aware of it, that's when I started to take action. I did not want my mismanagement to have a negative impact on what my family and my environment meant to me.

5 HOW I ACQUIRED BAD DEBTS AND FORGOT THE GOOD

First and foremost, I want to clarify what is the meaning of good debt and bad debt. It basically comes down to the following: the bad debt empties your pockets, leaving you with less money, and the good debt fills them and grows your income.

I will give you an example of bad debt (any of the ones I mentioned in the previous chapter would work), the example of buying a car by financing it. Buying a car means a capital outlay. In case you need it and if there is no other choice, you have to live with it since it's a need, and spend your money in one way or another. But buying a vehicle by financing it means that every month you have to pay a fee (this empties your pockets). And not just that, but that quota includes interest, which empties your pockets even more. Not to mention that it also has maintenance costs, the fuel expenses and taxes. All this empties your pockets exponentially since the acquisition of the car. This type of debt and all debts acquired impulsively, must be avoided at all costs. Bad debt is the one that will not bring you any economic benefit in the future. It is usually accumulated in credit cards, fast credits, credit for a trip, for a celebration, some electronic device, etc...They usually charge unreasonable interests.

And I take this opportunity to explain to you the "revolving method", that many credit cards use and that explains why it is so harmful to acquire this type of bad debt. The revolving card is the one that allows you, within your set limit, to split what you have purchased with it. They usually do this in two ways, or by setting a fixed fee to pay each month to gradually pay back what you've spent, or by setting a little % of what you owe (there are minimums and maximums). The problem with this method of payment is that it is subjected to exorbitant interest rates. When you're paying your monthly fee, you're actually paying mostly interests and very little of the principal (the debt when you buy with the Card). Avoid taking these methods of payment at all cost, or if you make use of them, cancel them as soon as possible, as they empty your pockets and also lengthen your debt for a long time without realizing it.

And going one step further, I want to mention Robert Kiyosaki's concept of "the rat race." I'll sum it up briefly, but for you to get an idea, first imagine the typical hamster that is on his wheel and that he has to go faster and faster to be able to continue on it. This concept alludes to the fact that we accumulate more and more debt, since we join the working world, as we tend to acquire debt to afford things like; a car, buy a house, get married, pay for a trip, buy furniture, a computer, etc... To do this, we increasingly need to work to be able to cope with all the payments and when we want to realize it, we are already immersed in a wheel where we are working to deal with the debts, which are getting bigger. In the end, we work harder to spend more. So, I advise you not to enter "the rat race" and if you are in, get out of it as soon as possible or at least minimize it as much as you can.

Let's move on to the good debt. This concept was something new for me. Nobody had taught me and, I hadn't thought about it either. The good debt, as I mentioned earlier, is the one that fills your pockets with money. And you'll say, how can that be possible if I'm taking on a debt. It's very simple, use that debt to invest it in something that will generate more money, greater than the own acquired by the debt. A simple example is a mortgage for a house. Not for your own use living in it, but with the purpose of renting it. The cost of the monthly mortgage must be lower than what you're getting for the rent. That is, if you have a mortgage of 600 euros and you rent it for 700 euros or more, the tenant will not only be paying for the mortgage, but you will also make an extra 100 euros. Consequently, you will be filling your pockets.

Good debt can be used to acquire assets that will be revalued in the future. This will generate revenue, which in turn if you invest it, will generate even more profits.

In general, it is usually better not to get into debts of any kind and make use of our own money. Although this statement is true, we will be acting well if we acquire good debt for a greater profit in the future, since we will not decapitalize our economy (using our savings) and we will be getting a return on that debt. This strategy is called" leverage," as you use money that isn't yours to help boost your investment. But if done, it must always be done using good debt. This way we will avoid being involved in an unwanted situation and very destructive to our private economy.

In conclusion, do all kinds of debt have to be eliminated? A priori, yes. And even more if it's bad debt. However, if the debt is to buy our own house, it is not a bad option since the interest is usually low and the amount of the mortgage is very high, normally not having enough savings to buy a house without getting into debt. We must always assess what it entails and calculate how it affects us.

Here I have explained and summarized it very quickly, but you can find books and videos on the internet that are more specific on this subject and talk about it more carefully and I advise you to learn more about these concepts. They're more important than they seem and it's worth spending some time learning about them. In my case, if I had known this before, I may have avoided some of the problems I came across.

6 EMOTIONS AND MONEY

When dealing with personal finances, we are required to mention emotions, as these are directly related. When we talk about money, we cannot ignore the fact that our relationship with it is intrinsically linked to our feelings. And this is more important than it seems. That is why I wanted to incorporate this section, to let you know that our emotions totally influence our way of managing money and how we feel when dealing with it. And if you check carefully, we are constantly dealing with money, every day, and pretty much for everything. It is the global exchange instrument. When we want to acquire something, the way to obtain it is usually through money. When it comes to personal development, if we want to do it at all levels, we must have a healthy relationship with everything around us. And if we really stop to think about it, money is something that is everywhere.

Our emotions are totally related to our consumption habits and learning how to manage them in regard to money is vital to grow as a person and have optimal financial health. There are different types of emotions when dealing with money, such as fear, shame or anger. There are already professionals in the field of behavioral finance, they are those who combine psychology with the private economy. They try to explain people's behavior when they decide to spend their money on one thing or another. So, we must always be attentive to our emotions when interacting with money. Only then we will be able to get to know ourselves better and manage our economy more consciously and in an appropriate way. If we ignore our feelings about money, we will probably end up frustrated, disappointed and having mismanaged our finances.

In general, most people when it comes to being linked to money, they often feel negative emotions, such as fear of losing their job, not being able to pay bills, comparing themselves to others having more money, having to make a big expense, etc... This ultimately translates into frustration and anger, which ultimately makes our relationship with money hateful. To get a good management of our finances, we must first have our emotions under control and change negative sensations and thoughts. To succeed in our economic management, we must change our mentality to a positive state towards money and then we will follow the steps to make such management possible.

Once we have identified the different emotions we have when dealing with money, the next thing to know is which kind of profile we have in an emotional level regarding money. This will help us to redirect our actions and thus lead us to get the results we are looking for at an economic level. Generally speaking, we can point out four types of profiles or as some call it, financial patterns. You will probably feel identified with one of them.

- Denial before money: These are people who see in money the source of all evil, they think

that money only brings problems.
- Money is synonymous of happiness: These are people who believe that money will solve all their problems and that is all they care about.
- Money reflects your social status: These are people who seek recognition from others through goods, the more and more expensive the better.
- Money controllers: These are people who prefer not to spend (excessively) and accumulate money, they are very afraid of spending.

And we must understand, that money alone is neither good nor bad. Money does not understand ethics, has no opinion, does not feel or suffer...money is just money. It's always going to depend on how we use it. In what we use it for and how we use it, is everyone's choice.

7 HOW TO MANAGE YOUR INCOME BETTER

I want you to learn how to manage your personal finances. That will mean you'll have more money and consequently you'll live more relaxed. To move towards financial freedom, you must first optimally manage your private economy. The first thing to do is to eliminate all kinds of debts. Second, systematic savings must be planned. And third, you have to invest that money or part of that money in sources of income. Here are the three basic steps you need to take to reach your financial freedom. All three can be linked and overlap each other, which means, it is not necessary to apply one after the other. I mean, it is not necessary to end the first step to start with the second, you can for example be eliminating debt and saving at the same time. There is the so-called Parkinson's Act, which says that "Expenses increase to cover all income", thus explaining why there is never money left even though incomes increase. The more we make, the more we spend. The more money we generate, the more we commit (financially) and this means that at the end of each month, we don't save. This is something we must avoid at all costs.

How to eliminate debt:

First, let's start by eliminating debts. That's in case you have them, as it happened to me, and as long as they're bad debts (as I explained in the previous chapter). There are different ways to eliminate our debts, but here I will explain what, in my opinion, is the most effective by far. It's easy to apply, motivates you and reduces debt-pending repayment time. It is the so-called "snowball effect" method and is applicable for any type of currency. The first thing you need to do is list out all your debts, and I emphasize all, even as small as it may seem. They can be credit cards debts, money you owe to an individual, personal credits, mortgage, car loans, furniture, electronics or whatever. That list has to be sorted by amounts, from lowest to highest, from the smallest pending debt to the debt you owe the most.

Example: order debts box

DEBT	MONTHLY FREE	TOTAL BALANCE
Cellphone payment	36 €	700 €
Credit card	60 €	1200 €
Car	300 €	14000 €
Mortgage	900 €	210000 €

lowest to highest

remaining balance

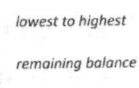

Once you have that listing and have your smallest debt in first position, what you have to do is to focus on it and settle it as quickly as possible. How? contributing an extra every month (by reducing some expendable expenses), as small as it may seem. That is to say, you pay the debt fee and you contribute an extra amount of money. This way you will speed up the return of it. I'll give you an example. If you have a total debt of 1000 euros, with a monthly fee of 100 euros (say at zero interest), you would be paying for 10 months until the debt is settled. Now let's say that each month in addition to the 100 euros you pay an extra of 50 euros. The result is that your debt is settled in 7 months and with a surplus of 50 euros.

Example: debt payment

CONVENTIONAL DEBT PAYMENT			PAYMENT WITH "SNOWBALL" METHOD		
MONTH	FEE	REMAINING	MONTH	FEE	REMAINING
1	100 €	1000 €	1	100 € + 50 € (extra)	1000 €
2	100 €	900 €	2	100 € + 50 € (extra)	850 €
3	100 €	800 €	3	100 € + 50 € (extra)	700 €
4	100 €	700 €	4	100 € + 50 € (extra)	550 €
5	100 €	600 €	5	100 € + 50 € (extra)	400 €
6	100 €	500 €	6	100 € + 50 € (extra)	250 €
7	100 €	400 €	7	100 € + 50 € (extra)	100 €
8	100 €	300 €	8	Time and interests saved	-50 € (surplus)
9	100 €	200 €	9		
10	100 €	100 €	10		

And now comes the core point. As you've already finished to settle your first debt, you move on to the second one on your list (the next smallest) and in addition to the monthly fee you pay, you'll advance each month the amount you were paying for the first debt , that is 150 euros. Hence it is called the "snowball effect", since each time the amount you return from each debt incurred is increased, which in turn reduces the repayment time. And consequently, you end up paying less interest and speeding up the payment process. Maybe at first it's hard to assimilate, at least it happened to me. The advantage is that there are many explanatory videos on the internet that can help you understand it perfectly. I recommend that if you have any doubts about applying the method entirely, you use those videos to gain knowledge and skills on how to apply it.

And you'll wonder, how do I get "extras" if I'm already having a hard time paying off all my debts and making it throughout the month. Well, I'll tell you some of the things that I did to get those "extras". I will give you two examples on how I managed to get some of my "extras": one was changing my coffee drinking habits (something I consumed in abundance), I stopped using coffee capsules of a reputable brand, to use a traditional coffee maker instead. And the reason behind it is that 3 coffee capsules cost approximately 30 coffee cups in a traditional coffee maker. So, it means that, with one coffee a day of capsules you can only consume for 3 days, however, with a traditional coffee maker, you can consume for 30 days (a whole month). A second example was eating out, we all like to go out and enjoy a meal, but most of the time we don't think about what that means. On average, the cost of a meal outside is equivalent to eating seven meals at home. It means that for a meal out, you can eat a whole week at home. Another way to get an extra that worked for me was instead of eating out four days a week, I would go three.

These "extras" can also be obtained through saving on the so-called "ant expenses", or micro expenses. These expenses are usually in our daily life almost without realizing it, and it is precisely because of their small amount that they go unnoticed. Hence, they go "eating" little by little our money. In fact, they represent as a whole a more significant sum than you might think. And I invite you to be aware of it and take some time to think and calculate how much it incurs. You can identify what habits you have and get that "extra" to eliminate debt (or save). Some of the most common "ant expenses" are: snacking at work, eating out, tobacco, alcohol, paid subscriptions, bank fees, coffees, gambling, candy, magazines, ice cream, etc.

The extras that you can reduce depend on you, according to your habits, customs or even addictions that we have often acquired and we do not consider how much they can cost us. It becomes beneficial and very profitable to take these into consideration and change our habits. There are other ways to reduce costs in order to get "extras". To me these were very effective, although you can also check your household consumptions (such as telephone rates, pay TV services, electricity and gas bills, insurance, etc...). The most effective thing is to combine several of them, so it will take less effort or your extra will be of greater amount. Combine them and you'll be optimizing your money and resources even more.

Savings Methods:

After you reduce and eliminate debt, the second thing you need to do is to plan on savings on a regular basis. There are basically two possible ways to save money; one is to reduce expenses and the other is to earn extra income.

The first is to calculate where you can cut from all your expenses so that you have a surplus for savings.

The second is to find an income alternative, such as a second job or a side job.

Saving, and having available the money that we have accumulated is essential to be able to face many of the situations that usually arise throughout our lives. In addition, it is a way to invest and make those savings, and ultimately our money, grow more every day. Saving is very important, not only because it is a basis for future investment, but it also allows us to have goals to acquire something we want. It also provides us with security, which translates into tranquility. And how to do it? Very simple, you have to incorporate habits into your life, in your day to day life to achieve it in an unconscious way, since once you have the habit implemented, it will not represent an effort anymore, and the benefits that saving will bring you will be great. Therefore, you have to systematically implement the savings.

There are many ways and many methods, so to make it easy for you, I will explain three of them, the ones I consider easier to implement and bring greater results. As Robert Kiyosaki says, pay yourself first. This means that if for example you have a job with a monthly payroll banked in your account, once you receive it, you must set aside an amount to a different account. To do this, you have to set a specific amount and give the automatic order to have that amount withdrawn each month. The amount that is usually recommended is between 10% to 20% of what you receive. Although this percentage depends on each one and their situation, I recommend that you set an amount that you can meet, not being a burden. It is better to start with a small percentage and increase it as you see that you can take more. For example, if you decide to save 10% and your income is €1000, once you receive your salary, you must have automatically set a transfer of €100 to another account. Therefore, your salary will become €900, from where you will deduct the mortgage or rent fee, car fee, receipts, etc ...but primarily is that from each payroll, you will have paid a part to yourself. This method is quite easy, since once you have implemented it, it is done automatically without having to worry again. Another method of saving is the so-called 52-week method. This method consists of each week of the year (which is 52), saving the amount of the number of the week you are in; the first week you have to save €1, the second week you have to save €2, the third week you have to save €3 and so on until you reach the last week of the year where have to save €52. Somehow it seems like an absurd method, but it's really simple and effective. At the end of the year you will find yourself having accumulated €1378, a more than a significant figure, since done otherwise, you will be probably spending this amount on other things without even realizing it.

As a final saving method, I'll explain the "three-thirds law." This concept as such comes from the Jews, who have it rooted in their culture and religion, and who are taught from childhood the importance of investing and prospering. From my side I will explain an adaptation aiming to save and invest at the same time. It involves any income you receive, dividing it into three parts, one part for all expenses, one part for saving and another part for investing. Depending on each person's situation, each part may vary in its percentage. A proportion that worked for me to begin with, and which I recommend you to carry out, was the 80/10/10. That is, of every income received, spend 80% on all your expenses (examples: mortgage, bills, food, clothes, etc.), 10% save it and deposit it in a separate account, having this way a contingency fund (this means having a "financial buffer" to face any unforeseen or extra expense). The other 10% allocate it for investments, being this the money that will be growing increasingly in the medium-long-term run (examples: in investment funds, a business, in the stock exchange, etc...)..

Example: "Three-Thirds Law" to Begin with (80/10/10)

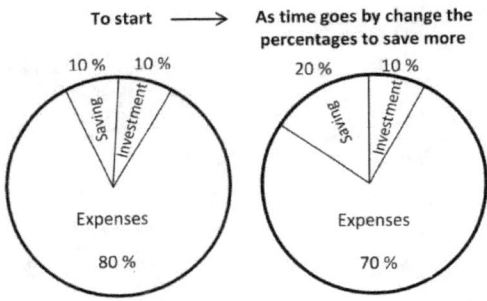

This investment, which I will discuss in the next chapter, will ultimately lead you to generate even greater profits and will help you achieve financial freedom. The percentage set into three parts must then change, by 70/20/10 for example, and thus increase the savings a little more and allocate less to expenses. Once you've been applying this formula for a while and have considerable savings, I advise you to stop saving and assign the percentage allocated to saving for investments. Yes, stop saving and switch to investing. To do this, I recommend that your savings are about one-third of your annual net income. Therefore, if for example you earn 20,000 euros per year, once you have saved 6,500 euros, stop saving and allocate this percentage towards investments. This way, having reached this point, you will have a contingency fund (the 6,500 euros saved), deep-rooted planning habits in your economy, and the chance to invest and grow your money. At this point your percentages might start as follows:

Example "Law of the Three-Thirds" focused on INVESTING

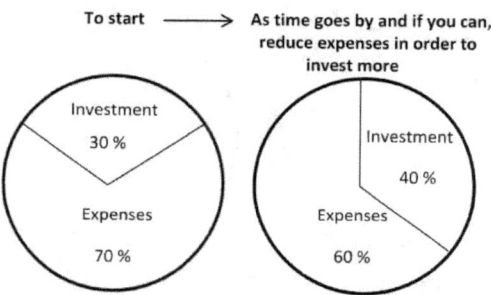

Investment:

The investment, that unknown matter to some but rather overlooked by many others in our private economy management. And the main reason is fear. Fear is the worst enemy for investment, for our money growth and ultimately to become financially free. It paralyzes us, preventing any chance of taking risks, stopping us from moving forward. It is partly because of the way we have been raised, under the idea of fear of money, rather than seeing it as it is; a fundamental vehicular tool that allows us to acquire and achieve what we want. The investment is largely based on wanting to take a change and get us out of our comfort zone. That is why, so many people avoid investing. So, the first thing to do is to break that fear, always assume a calculated risk, even if it's a small one and risk. When talking about investment, I am not saying to take any chance unknowingly. Obviously when investing, firstly you have to understand well, spend time learning, value the pros and cons and once this is done, assume it or not. Do it in a way that is "comfortable" for you and does not end up being an ongoing anguish. This is up to each person.

Before I go into this section, I want to introduce you to some terminologies that will help you understand how to invest. We all understand the meaning of what income is and what expenses are. In general, it's the revenue that fills our pocket of money and the expenses are the ones that empty it.

Now, I want to focus on income (all the money we receive) and we can generate it in two different ways; one is actively (it means that we receive money for example from investing our time at work, whether working as an employee or getting paid for each job we do, investing our time in each of them), the other way is to receive income passively. This is the type of income I want to focus on, passive income (it means we get money automatically, without having to do anything, for example receiving an amount of money for the rental of a parking space that we own, we do nothing and every month we receive an amount of money).

On the other hand, there are expenses. We can spend our money on things that won't get us anything (profit wise) in return in the future (for example a cell phone, you buy it and then it will never give you a benefit) or on the contrary we can spend our money on things that in the future will generate money (for example, buy a commercial store and then rent it). This is a type of investment, spending on something that will generate money for us in the future. That initial "expense" will become in the future passive income. In short, an investment. What you consider today an expenditure, if it is in something that in the future will generate income, it is actually called an investment.

The goal of the investment I want you to achieve is to capitalize on your money to boost its value in the future. Whether it's increasing your net worth or getting returns on assets you purchase. Assets are in everything you've spent (invested) that will then generate money for you. So, the sequence is as follows: you receive an income, spend part of it buying assets that will generate money passively, therefore now you will have invested and will be making money.

After showing you these different concepts, let's get to the key question: where to invest. Well, before you ask that question, the first thing you need to know is which kind of "investor" you are. There are people who are willing to take on more risk than others, some are more conservative and some are willing to take the risk and lose if things go wrong. Depending on which investment you go for, you can lose. The good part is that no one forces you to do anything and it will always be you, and only you, who decides what to do with your money and how to invest it. Here I will mention different ways to invest in assets that will generate passive income. Obviously, you could generate income in a different way like getting a second job, creating something and selling it, teaching, anything you could charge for and get an income. One way to invest is to generate revenue from something you know how to do. It's investing in yourself. Make your talent a source of income. I'm sure there's something you're good at, something you do better than others. Take advantage of it and obtain an economic return.

Here I will tell you some of the methods that I implemented into practice to generate passive income. To begin with, and having in mind the simple goal of fighting inflation (which broadly means that the money you have today, in a few years, the same amount will be worth less because the price of things will be higher), you have to move your money, if it stays static it will lose value in the future. You must place it somewhere that will benefit you in the medium-long term, such as a well-advised banking product, invest in the stock market, allocate it to a business, buy a property, etc... (learning about it and having no doubts about what you are hiring or purchasing). I have never really liked banking products, as these are intended to mainly benefit banks. But in a way they can be "used" to monetize your savings.

Before we go any further, let me tell you something that seems obvious, you don't have to know everything. The most important thing is to know who to entrust the task you need to do and therefore someone to do it for you, knowing beforehand that they will perform it successfully because they master the subject and they do it for a living. That is why specialties, technicians and professions exist. Take advantage of it and ask for what you need for, whenever you need it. In other words, when your kitchen sink breaks down, you can try to fix it yourself, if you are able to and have some skills, or you can call a plumber either to fix it or explain to you how to settle it. The same thing happens with money, for instance if at any time you want to invest in the stock market, you can do it on your own or delegate it to a consultant. You can also get training and do it yourself. But what I mean by this is that you don't need to be a specialist in everything, you just have to know and choose well where to search for and who to ask.

That being said, another way to invest is to buy an asset that generates fully passive income. As mentioned earlier, purchasing an apartment and renting it out (provided your situation allows you to do so and you have another place to live), or a parking space, or a storage, a piece of real estate that will become profitable. These generate revenue periodically without having to do anything actively. Another way of investment is creating a product or service that does not require your time (or basically does not require much of your time). You make an initial effort to create something (for example a book, an online course, a tutorial on a specific topic) and once it's done, when you market it (sell it) it will start generating revenue without having to invest more time, effort or money (if applicable) in it. In terms of offering a service, it usually requires more time and follow-up, but if you can combine it with your day-to-day life, it will always be an additional source of revenue.

And once listed the different sources of income, I would like to highlight a concept; diversifying. This in terms of investment refers to you allocating your investments in different areas. This will lead you to not only have one source of income, but to have several sources. No matter the amount, the important thing is to generate as much profit as possible with different assets. So, if one investment fails or falls shorter, it will be compensated with the one that works best or works very well. We can avoid putting all the eggs in the same basket, since it is always riskier this way.

In terms of investing, we should not have the cliché of a stock market investor, which is also an option, but as you can see there are many other ways to "invest" in order to generate an income. All in all, keep your money moving and it will increase. Because stationary money, will always lose value. So, invest, and invest in yourself and for yourself. Because once you start, it does all come around and all the invested efforts will be rewarded, I assure you. The day will come when you will start to see results (profitability) and when that happens, it will mean two things, the first thing is that you will know that you are on the right track, and the second thing is that you will no longer be able to stop, you will have learned to invest and you will not stop doing it anymore.

8 TOWARDS FINANCIAL FREEDOM

I have to confess that, until recently, I did not know what the concept of financial freedom was. Worst of all, it hadn't even crossed my mind. I hadn't even thought about it. Of course, I wasn't taught this subject, and I hadn't even heard of it. So, I couldn't have set that goal, not having this source of inspiration to get it. I see it as something so important that I think it can change the lives of a lot of people, not only economically speaking, but change the way and lifestyle we decide to have. Because yes, it's a choice, it's within our power to choose to follow one path or another. We choose the kind of life we want to lead. I took that direction, and you, reading this, have done it too. Now don't stop, don't give up and go down this path.

To achieve financial freedom, first, and I emphasize first, what you need to do is to invest in financial education, I can't tell you more clearly. Read, attend conferences, take courses, watch videos, etc... Everything about financial education. Anything that can give you knowledge about personal finance management. Knowledge will set the way to your goal. Learn, learn and don't stop learning. We're never going to be able to know everything, but even when we fail and get it wrong, we learn. Don't ever stop training, because the more you learn and better informed you are, the more you realize how much you have left to learn.

The formula you need to implement to achieve financial freedom is to purchase as many assets as you possibly can, and let these assets generate passive income. So, you have to invest. Gather these types of assets until you reach your goal. Then, if you want to, you can stop working. Or not...and you will work on something that also generates income actively, but you will be able do it without worrying about the economic part and dedicate yourself to what you want and like. The key is being able to choose and that is priceless. The power of choice, in a truly free way, that's the prize you'll receive. You will achieve something huge, not only economically, but also on a personal level.

Believe me, regardless in which situation you are at this moment, you can choose to change your attitude and focus on the same goal that I set myself. I don't want you to stay still after reading this book, I want you to move towards your own financial freedom.

Wherever you are right now, according to a Chinese proverb, "the best time to start investing was 25 years ago, the next best time is now." Think that you are not going to lose anything and what you can earn is seriously great. Do it because you will never regret having followed the path towards your true freedom. Find a strong motivation, a specific goal to achieve and you will succeed.

Apply the steps mentioned in this guide, eliminate debt (if you have it, if you don't, then it will be much easier and faster to reach your goal), implement a savings system and invest. This way you'll make your money grow, you will grow as a person, and you be on your way to your own financial freedom.

9 SUMMARY OF CONCEPTS:

1. Financial freedom: can be defined as a person's ability to meet all of their economic needs without having to work. Related to financial freedom is term "passive income" as the source of income that does not require any activity to receive money.

2. Financial education: is the ability to understand how money is used in the world, how a person obtains (earns) it, manages it, invests it and donates it to help others. More specifically, financial education refers to the set of skills and knowledge that allow an individual to make informed decisions of all their financial resources.

3. Good debt: it is the one that allows us to purchase an asset that in the future will bring us a benefit. For example, buying a home, creating a business, or training.

4. Bad debt: it is the one we incur to purchase goods that we don't normally need or that we can't afford. For example, making use of credit cards that employ the "revolving method" which makes the debt endless and results in huge interest.

5. Ant expenses or micro expenses: Those small expenses in the day to day life that are "eating" our money so little by little that we do not even realize, but that actually involves a considerable expense.

6. "Snowball "effect: it is the method to apply in order to eliminate quickly the debt that we have incurred, resulting paying less interest and having more money each month.

7."The Rat Race": alludes to the fact that we are accumulating more and more debts, to pay for things like; a car, buy a house, get married, pay for a trip, buy furniture, a computer, etc... That leads us to need to work harder to be able to cope with all the payments, which are getting bigger.

8. **Link between emotions and money:** it is a fact that our emotions are directly linked to how we handle money. Our emotions are totally related to our consumption habits and learning how to manage them regarding money is vital to grow as a person and to have optimal financial health.

9. Savings methods: One, to set a fixed amount each month of our income and save it in a separate account. Two, to implement the 52-week method (we'll save every year 1378 euros). Three, to apply the "three-thirds law" that best suits our situation, for example start with 80/10/10.

10. Assets: these are valuable resources that we must purchase with the goal of generating profits in the future.

11. Passive income: it is to get money automatically, without having to do anything, for example entering an amount of money when renting our own parking spot.

12. Importance of investing: only investing you will manage to multiply your money, and hence you can become financially free. Invest in financial education, invest in purchasing assets and invest in yourself.

13. Inflation: inflation reflects the loss in purchasing power, what means that the same amount of money today (for example 1000 euros), will be worth less in 5 years from now if you do not put means for it to grow.

14. Optimize your time: make use of your knowledge and skills to make money. Make profitable what you know to generate income.

15. Parkinson's Law: this one says that "Expenses increase to cover all income", thus explaining why there is never money left even if the income increases. The more we make, the more we spend.

16. Diversify: This in terms of investment refers to you dividing your investment in different areas. This will lead you to not only have a source of income, but to have several, regardless of the amount. The important thing is to generate as much profit as possible from different assets.

10 RECOMMENDATIONS:

If you found this book interesting, useful and helpful, (hopefully it did) I will then have achieved my goal, I invite you to read the following books and thus enhance your knowledge. They are as follows:

- Rich Dad, Poor Dad (Robert Kiyosaki)
- The Richest Man in Babylon (George S. Clason)
- The Money Code (Raimon Samsó)
- Tu llave a libertad financiera (Esmeralda Gómez López)
- Financial Freedom in two steps (Agustin Grau)
- 30 Days, change your Habits, Change your Life (Marc Reklau)
- Ten peor coche que tu vecino (Luis Pita)
- The monk who sold his Ferrari (Robin Sharma)
- Money Master the Game (Tony Robbins)
- The Luck Factor (Richard Wiseman)
- The Intelligent Investor (Warren Buffet)

There are many others, but if you start with these, you'll have a good base. They helped me a lot to get on the road to becoming financially free. In fact, I will be financially free, and it will be partly thanks to all of them, among many others, including you. So, thank you.

ABOUT THE AUTHOR

I was born in Barcelona in 1985 to a humble working-class family. I graduated from high school, and in addition to learningbout Financial Education, I have a full-time job.

My goal is to achieve financial freedom and I want to help others improve their personal finances.

I have acquired extensive knowledge about economic management and, together with my personal experiences, all this knowledge led me to want to teach others about all the good that can be achieved with healthy economic habits.

You will be able to learn more about me on my website, I invite you to look it up. I will also share with you different links of interest, I will recommend books that will help you, and you will be able to ask me any questions you like: **www.lectiofinanzas.com**

www.ingramcontent.com/pod-product-compliance
Lightning Source LLC
Chambersburg PA
CBHW070831220526
45466CB00002B/797